1613 elmwood

Stanley's Son

A Life's Journey

Harris David Foster

STANLEY'S SON
A LIFE'S JOURNEY

iUniverse books may be ordered through booksellers or by contacting:

iUniverse
1663 Liberty Drive
Bloomington, IN 47403
www.iuniverse.com
1-800-Authors (1-800-288-4677)

ISBN: 978-1-4917-7846-3 (sc)
ISBN: 978-1-4917-7847-0 (e)

Print information available on the last page.

iUniverse rev. date: 10/16/2015

Foreword

I never expected this book to be completed in such rapid fashion. During the past year, both my parents died, I received medical treatment for cancer and other ailments and experienced the abrupt end of a relationship.

All these challenges have given rise to the following pages. I am grateful for how well my first book, "A Way Home" was received by my dear friends and colleagues.

If we think about it, we have all had "life changing" events in our lives. I had two significant emotional breaking points, one in October of 2014 and one in March 0f 2015. I found myself hanging by a thread emotionally. It was my friends who "talked me down" from the ledge. I am so blessed to have these loving, kind and accepting people in my life. I would have never survived without them. So with great love and respect I honor:

John Daubney

Rob/Joanne Reeves

Gary Enright

Janice Stavros

Judy Prichason

Candy McLeod

Grace Foster

Dina Jameson

Dedication

To My Parents

Stanley "Red" Foster
April 1, 1924 – May 14, 2014
Bella "Bubbie" Foster
September 12, 1924 – March 14, 2015

Memorial

Beau Biden
(Vice President Biden's Son)

Dr. Wayne Dyer
(Author/Lecturer)

James Horner
(Composer Conductor)

Gary Richrath
(Guitarist, REO Speedwagon)

Table of Contents

The Choice

There is a choice when you love
You invest your heart and soul
In time you share
You give and take

There is choice when you weep
Your emotions climb
They must escape
You go down and reflect

There is a choice to forgive
Your caustic words cause a slice
Maybe to speak with a filter is best
You ask for forgiveness

There is a choice to let go
Your body is burdened with grief
You must lay down
You turn to the heavens and chant

Your choice is to heal
Your wounds bleed with sorrow
You recover from another
If not in your time

So turn it over
Let it go
And know the begin day begins again

Perfection

There are a very few things that are perfect
A snowflake descending in its fall
The angelic face of an infant
The rainbow that garnishes the sky
The calm waters of a tranquil lake

No man can be perfect
No man can be without a foible
No man can be above reproach
No man should be worshiped
No man can have all the answers

We are imperfect beings
We are afforded with flexibility
We learn again if we choose
We love at random
We humble ourselves often

Perfection is unworthy of spent time
Perfection prevents us from swaying to our own song

Pyramid Lake, NY

The Road Ends

The car knows the way to the end of the road
The winding gravel pattern aligned with mighty pines
The scent of sap swirls about in concert
I find myself high with anticipation

Then I drive no further
I must walk up the hill to greet the heavenly body
She waits for me in every season
My great spiritual constant

I float on the winds
It holds me up
It send me in all direction with tranquil silence

The paddle dips in cadence
The boat slithers through the glistening waters
Then I stop for every reason
To inhale, marvel, inhale

I am in awe
Time stands still
My beating heart knows peace and serenity

Discard

One cannot throw away love
It is like gum on your shoe
Once cannot out run love

Love is not of touch
Love is not of words
Love is not of poems
Love is not of songs

Love is all around us
Without shape, unbreakable and sturdy
Love surrounds us like a warm embrace
Love shapes us like a sculpture's hand

So let love flow
Let go where it finds you

Nacht

These days I dread the night
It is not the darkness I fear
Nor think the ghosts might get me

The darkness taints my soul
It darkens my spirit
It causes me to toss and turn inside and out
It leaves my head in a fever of confusion

My thoughts have been hijacked by a speeding train
I wish I could jump off
I wish I could break my fall

I did not always have this terror.....

I used to dream of angels singing
I used to dream of vibrate colors
I used to dream of calm water
I used to dream of her and her so close

Then she slipped away
Finding her way to another
Giving his night that was once was mine

I have to find my way through the night
To pray my way through this monster
To fall asleep sometime soon
An awaken to the healing light of tomorrow

Hold Me

Would you dance with me?
May I hold you close?
Let the music help us sway in time

Very soon we will move as one
Our feet gliding across the floor
I may softly sing to you
I may kiss your cheek

After the music ends
Dance with me
Let my heart beat keep us in time
Let our breath remind us of life

After we part
Please know I will keep dancing
My heart will still beat to the music

Crash

I was hit by a bus the other day
It ran me over

I boarded a plane
It crashed and left me in pieces

I jumped out of a plane
The parachute didn't open

I boarded a boat
It sprung a leak

I mounted a horse
It had no shoes

I sat in a chair
It had only three legs

I should have stayed home
Locked the door
I should have not run away

Ends This

Please put an end to my suffering
Please make it all go away

The hours of pain are unrelenting
The nights feel like years

I pace the floors in disarray
I am exhausted having climb Everest twice

Why is this happening to me?
What have I done so wrong to bear this sentence?

I feel like I am dying
Slowly

Stanley's Last Car

Used Car

She could not afford a new car
So she found a used one

It seemed to run well
All the parts were finely tuned

She liked its comfort
She felt safe even as a passenger

She took three short trips
One for dinner
One for pizza and a film
One walk by the canal

The without warning
She left the car on the side of road
She vanished, never to be heard of again

There is a rumor she is looking for a new car

Stuck

On a fall afternoon
I make my way through the carpet of fallen leaves
The colors of the trees provided to set the scene

Making my way around the still lake at Mercer
I stop for a rest by the water
I look out at the loons floating with such grace
I inhale many times, the intoxicating breeze

I am overcome with emotion
The beauty of the moment
I am witness to nature's perfection

The tears rise to cloud my vision
Deep to the bone it travels
I feel everything

I move closer to the water's edge
And deposit my tears

5 Years

It is half a decade
It is longer than a presidential term
Over 15,000 days

During the time they lit up my face
They gave me a glow that can be seen at night
They cut my flesh to find some more
They fed me poison with uncertain consequences

I gave my body away a long time ago
What they cannot take is my will

So I press on
I hope
I fight, even on the days when I cannot muster the will

Bottom Line

Given the choice I would rather be in love
It is worth the risk to open the heart
To hand her the keys

Given the choice I would rather have passion
It is a hand to hold, a tender kiss and a kind word
To touch is to promise

Given the choice I would rather have commitment
To make a promise with one to go all in
To vow to be dedicated to one heart

Given the choice I would rather have closeness
The warm embrace, feeling her heart beat
To be one with another

The choice is mine

Vice Grip

Sometimes I hold on to tight
My knuckles turn white
My hands ache

What feeds the grip is fear
Being unable to let go
Knowing the emptiness that follows

To hold onto a heart with tension
Is to deprive the beat of hope
To embrace a lover to close
Is to stunt reciprocation

To hold to tightly over time
Will cause a death
A passing of unlimited possibilities

So I have a dilemma
I presented with options
To let go
To ease off
To pain less

To gift myself......hope

Gardens of Stone

I was restless the other night
I was startled to see her at the foot of my bed
I remembered her instantly surrounded in a silhouette of bright light

She said to me that they were saving a place for me
Where all the family was residing
She said they were finally all happy and getting along quite well

She said things were different now
All the judgement and anger was gone
She said he wouldn't criticize me any more
She said he would say kind words to me
She said he would watch me pitch
She said he would stay at the table for all the meals
She said he was sorry for what happened
She said he did the best he could

She said they no longer worshiped money instead of G-d
She said she wouldn't close the door in my face
She said she would love me unconditionally
She asked me to forgive her for not protecting me
She got down on her knees

I thought about all she had said
So much information to digest from a lifetime
My response was …..
I have traveled a long road
I have visited high peaks
I have groveled in low places

I have howled in pain like a wolf in the night
I have marched through my struggles
I have witnessed the beauty of nature
I have witnessed the birth of my beautiful child
I have leaned on my deep faith
I value my "chosen" family

I granted us forgiveness
Stating I am building my own home brick by brick
One day at a time

Gratitude

These are days where nothing goes right
When each decision I make goes horribly wrong
When my worries cause a restless night
When my girl goes away to another

These are days when I question
Where is my life going and does it have meaning
When I desire what I cannot have
When my emptiness cannot be filled

These are the days when I wonder how much time I have wasted
Procrastination I hear is the thief of time
When I feel all those things
The last thing I want to recognize is gratitude

Gratitude helps me disconnect from
Fear
Uncertainty
Emptiness

It fills me with opportunity
It gives me hope

Unloved

They would secretly say that loving is all that matters
It is the essential feeling that sustains a beating heart

Many wait years to meet that one ignites a spark
Though hard to explain but easy to identify in that moment
It is a feeling like no other
Many stories, poems and songs try to describe

It is a meeting of two souls
It as much unspoken language as deep intimate conversation
And then without reason the well goes dry
The heart grows cold
The look of adoration turns to distain

The party that stays is devastated
Left to sweep up the pieces
Shattered like glass

They tell him it takes time to put the pieces back together
He needs to heal
To vent his agony

How much time?
How many darken nights?
How much time on his knees?

How long does it take to unlove ?

Bella Foster (c 1979)

Cook

I know my way around the kitchen
I can find any utensil with great accuracy
I can cut, chop and dice with the best of them

I can prepare a meal with patience and dedication
I know all the steps sometimes not following a plan
I like an audience when I cook

To engage in any conversation
Perhaps some wine
Maybe a song
A rest to kiss the cook

Then as the warmth of the kitchen takes over
It is time to present the creation
Candles set the stage
The aroma is intoxicating
The company even better

Before the first bite
We join hands to express grace
We commune with food
Prepared with love and kindness

May it enrich us
May it provide us with
Peace
Comfort
And Love

Go Back

I would be lying if I said I didn't desire
To transport myself back in time
To redo undo things

Today I am much more aware
Things are much clearer
My feelings are so relevant
I am a better man

I would find those people
I would speak my truth
They need not apologize, just to listen
I would confront the witch and bring my bucket

Then I would find her
I would hold her face in my hands
I would just stare at that joyous picture

Those eyes that lit my soul
That smile that elevated my heart
We would speak again without words

I would give thanks for the visit
To realize when I have been
How far I have come today

As tomorrow awaits me with unlimited possibilities

Pyramid Lake Men's Retreat (1992)

Friends

Over a lifetime they find a way into my life
Some remain as a constant beacon of hope
Some stay for only a brief moment

These are people who share a common thread
These are people who are of good standing
These are people who have a great capacity to love

No matter what time of day
No matter what season
No matter how I feel
They appear

My friends are the greatest gift to me
They require nothing of me
They ask for nothing in return
They know at any time
I will be there for them

During the darkest hours
When deprived of sleep
I feel their hand on my heart
They provide light when in despair

My friends except me as the man I am
With all my foibles and defects
They are my greatest blessing

Blindness

All along she was standing right in front of me
I did not see her

All along she professed her love to me
I didn't hear her

All along she wanted to pray with me
I never took her

All along she wanted to dance with me
I never heard the music

All along she wanted me to sing to her
I became mute

Now she is gone
I hear her to late
I saw her to late
I spoke to late
I have no chance to engage her

I was blind by my own wounds
I was afraid to love her
I was afraid to unlock my heart
To grant her passage

She is gone…

Stanley's Son

Why Wait

What are you waiting for?
The phone to ring?
A knock at the door?
A compliment?
Validation?

You could sit still and watch the hands move
You could watch the light change to darkness
You could sit and chant

Would have
Could have
Should have

You would be a fool
Time waits for no one, not even you
You would be wasting your life

So get up
Keep moving
Avoid the decent into self-loathing

Affirm who you are
Affirm that you have value
And know that you are a precious gift

The Victim

To be a victim is to sign up and volunteer
To be a victim is to self injure
A victim holds self hostage

Feeling the pain of
Disappointment
Loss
Abandonment
Betrayal
Is perfectly relevant to the human condition
But one must set the time to be free to
Emote
Weep
Purge

To construct a documentary or mini-series of suffering
Will always stunt the healing process

So set the timer
Create a concrete end

The continuous victim is bore
Failing to quiet the enlarged ego

Dina and Hannah (c. 1995)

Stanley's Son

Carry Her

Her tiny feet make small trails on the damp sand
In the distance she sees the ocean blue
The east coast and west coast could be identical twins

Soon her short legs grow tired
She turns to her mother with arms extended
She is then scooped and carried off the hip

They continue to the waters' edge
Though calm but too cold to enter
The breeze brushes their hair

Throughout our lives we carry our children
As they become more agile and weighted
They walk beside us
We then hold a hand

When they become older the hand grows cold
But we always carry their spirit in our heart

Stanley's Son

Mend

In the song they ask a question?
How do you mend a broken heart?

A transplant is not a viable option
A few stiches and some duct tape just will not suffice
What options are then available?

Perhaps one would be to lie with another
Forget the lover who is now with another
Perhaps another would be to accept all the pain
To put your face in a gust of wind
Just grit your teeth and bear it
Take it, embrace it, howl and curse the heavens
Get down on your knees and humble yourself
Simply surrender

Then each day will heal you
Each sunrise with fuel the spirit
Each evening will sooth your soul
Each day will present a new door to open

To mend a broken heart
Takes time
Not in your time
In time

Hammered

My head hurts
Time and time again
I hit myself

I strike myself with
Doubt
Insecurity
Fear
Projection
Shame

I grab the handle and WACK !!

The results are the same
The lesson not learned
I am chasing my tail

I need to step away
Place the hammer back in the tool box

West Witch

I met her just once
She said she wanted to be swept off her feet
I bought her a broom
And then she flew away

To Rise Above

What is our true challenge in life?
What are those things that leave us confounded?
Who are those individuals that cause us angst?
What unexpected events throw us off kilter?

A man of insight might tell you to look no further
Find a mirror and tell me what you see
Do not turn away in shame
Open your eyes and see who you really are
Refrain from self-judgment

Then begin the journey
Be prepared to find confusion, sadness and doubt
Do not give into fear
Do not turn away from you
To avoid the pain and the broken
Is to deny our existence
Be courageous and face the fire
Feel the heat of change
Embrace the dying embers

Then remember everything changes
With every new sunrise is a new beginning
Die to the past
Stand in the present
Live in the moment

The power lies within each of us

Stanley's Son

Move On

They all tell me the same thing
Move on

In theory they are right
The head seems to be enlightened

The heart has other plans
Each part is important to follow
They are in clear conflict

The heart feels
The head thinks

The heart races with passion
The head calms with thought

The heart is tender remembering the touch
The head is driven by practical matters

There are no winners nor losers in this battle
It all comes down to what I decide

To trust the feelings
To go all in
It is my call

Unreturnable

I was given something I did not ask for
I was given a challenge that I was drafted into

I had to time to rehearse
I had no time to prepare
I had no time to edit the script

So I took what they gave me
I accepted with great hesitation

I felt devastating fear
I experienced monumental uncertainty
I even tried negotiating a deal with my maker
It was all for naught

I took my medicine
I took the burning
I took the drilling
I took the probing
I took the poison

All for the chance to live

Naked

The truth has no clothes
The lies are over dressed

Speaking your truth means opening your soul
Speaking your truth provides you with ultimate freedom

Getting to that point is a challenge
Getting to trust your gut takes time

Staying silent provides little outlet
Staying stuck leaves you paralyzed

It all comes down to choice
It all comes down to not asking for permission

It is the ultimate freedom
So unshackle your being
So speak your truth
Be not influenced by others voices
Never imagine the consequences

That would be like reading the last chapter of the book first

Stanley's Son

Resilience

To bounce back
To get up when you're knocked down on your ass
To live another day
To go to work when you would rather stay in bed
To turn the other cheek
To error and admit it
To apologize and mean it
To speak up despite the consequences

You can lick your wounds
But you will be back

Never quit!!

Justin Hayward

Stanley's Son

Good Medicine

I am not sure what comes first?
The music or the lyrics
For those that collaborate as a duet
For those who perform solo
I am in awe of their talents

When I hear the music it washes over me like a spring shower
When I hear the words they speak just to me like the voice of angels

The music has been a soundtrack to my life
When I hear a tune I am transported to that moment
It is exactly where I am
It precisely what I am feeling
It is as if time stood still

The music ignites my emotional fire
It stokes my passion
It sets ablaze my soul
It warms my heart
My soul is radiant

Through all my feelings, the music takes my emotions for a ride
Through all my sadness, the words facilitate tears
Both of angst and joy

I trust all the tunes
They speak in a language of hope
A promise of a better day

Music is the most powerful medicine
It provided me with endless refills

The Power

It was right in front of my nose
A blind person would have found it
A young child could easy point it out

I was blind
I was unaware
I was misinformed

I had the keys to the car but forgot how to drive
I had all the directions but kept getting lost
I even had a GPS but was to stubborn to plug it in
I even refused a call from Dorothy

Then over time I began to see
My vision became intuitive
I moved forward with decisiveness

I have the power to change only ME
I have the power to learn new ways
I have the power to live my life on my terms.

Free Will

We all have been given a great gift
It has little monetary value
It is something you cannot grasp
It is something one cannot see

It gives us great freedom
It allows us to blaze our own path
It helps us feel unique

We can use it at will
It will never spoil
It has no expiration date

We have choices in life
The opportunities are limitless
The rewards can be glorious

What are you waiting for?

Good Practice

Each day provides me a way to heal
Each sunrise reminds me of a new birth of the spirit
Each dusk is rewarded for a day well lived

My pain is beginning to recede like the oceans tide
My ability to see where I have been is clear
My insight as to how I lost my way is apparent

I feel a sense of freedom
I feel light on my toes
I am humbled by where I have been

So I died to the relationship
I mourned the loss
I have managed to navigate the high seasons of emotions

So just for today
I see the sunshine on even the cloudiest of days
I embrace the night as a reward for a good day

One step
One day
At a time

Recant

I made a terrible mistake
I want to take back every word
I stated I was ready to go, my bags were packed

I said I would answer the call and leave immediately
I would be leaving behind those I loved
What was I thinking?
How could I be so self-involved?

If I left now
So many things would be missed
The change of season
The ocean's tide
The scent of grass
The falling snow
The aroma of my culinary delights
A tender kiss
A warm hand to hold
A warm embrace

I was misled by my own gratification
I fooled myself in thinking I was "done"
I still have much to do
I still desire to make a difference
I still want to live.

Stanley's Son

Words

It is much easier to write when the pain surrounds me
The words flow with such a tsunami force
Nights of uncertain sleep turns into literary gifts

And then over time joy pays a visit
I often find great discomfort in the calm
The goodness that has taken me over is uncomfortable
Like wearing a new pair of shoes

But sometimes the words take a vacation
I search for them without success
These words should not be forced with discomfort

As joy and pleasure envelop me
The loss of words leaves me confused and empty
To be happy and joyous is unsettling
The conflict between these two states is confusing

I have lived with the distrust of both good and decent
That in a blink of an eye
It will vanish
That I should not trust it

So my charge is to embrace happiness though uncomfortable
To hold to every joyous second and bathe in the pleasure
I believe in time the words will replenish my soul

The 51 State

Wide and diverse is the space we occupy
In all directions we reside

Some of us reside by the coast
Some by the mountains
And some in the Great Plains

In the state that we live we call it home
A place where we find peace and comfort

But at times we live in another state
A sparsely populated place

It is not a tangible place
It is not made of terrain nor landscape

It is a place deep inside of us
Maybe a section of the soul
That allows us a state of calm

It may provide us with gratitude and peace
It may humble us when we need silence
It may speak to us without interruption

To reside in a state of grace
Is to live in a state of humility

To send the ego on a sabbatical

The Crack in the Door

Most of the time the door of yesterday is closed
There are moments when I look back with great joy
Those stolen moments that brightened my day

Yesterday's joy also brings the pain of today
Those moments from the past ignite my sorry
I need to keep then in perspective
I need to honor them

I am a fool to believe she will return
The handle does not turn
The phone does not ring
The glowing face I admire so has vanished

But on occasion I am triggered to open the door a crack
I am tempted by feelings of abandonment
I am overwhelmed with deep sadness

When we shared so much
We laughed so loudly
When laid together
Time stood still

I allow myself to miss her
I grieve the loss
My tears will heal me

Fear

How can one word paralyze the masses?
Its meaning is fueled by the unknown
To project the outcome is a waste of time

But what if we were all mistaken
But what if we gave false energy to just a mere four letters
But what if we took back the control we so easily gave away

To let go is initially painful
It will cause us to fidget
It would cause a temporary restlessness

In time it would pass through us
We soon feel unburdened
We would be free to make choices
We would give us the freedom to live

Fear is like a stop sign
One must approach it with caution
Then apply the breaks
Remember to look both ways

Then move ahead

More Gratitude

Let us sing in praise for gratitude
Let us acknowledge what we have
Let us suppress the desire for more
Let us pronounce

"I HAVE ENOUGH"

In those moments when we feel desperation
Let us give gratitude
When we cry out in the night and feel alone
Let us give gratitude
When nights feel like an eternity
Let us give gratitude

When we go down
Let us give gratitude
When tears overwhelm us
Let us give gratitude
When our lover leaves us
Let us give gratitude
When death takes them away
Let us give gratitude

When we are accepted for who we are
Let us give gratitude
When someone takes are call
Let us give gratitude
When someone offers a hand to hold
Let us give gratitude

To give gratitude is to pay homage to who we are

Female Hero

With the very best intentions they marry
Based on a foundation of love and respect
Unaware of the secrets of the past
That lay smoldering under the surface

As the years pass, his eye begins to wander
His touch grows cold
He soon see her as invisible
The passion fades like the morning dew
She cries inside every night

Then she makes a deal to stay
For the sake of the children
Years pass the wall between them grows taller
He cheats, lies and steals
He rages, both with hands and words
She retreats and tends to the children
She surrenders to hopelessness

But then a miracle appears
An epiphany
She has reached her limit
She packs him up and out he goes

She is courageous but fearful
She has doubt but is hopeful
She wants to be held
She wants to be respected

She is her own hero

Stanley's Son

Shadow Pain

I know what you have been through
I have walked in your shoes
I have felt the drenching tears shower me

I have fallen to the depths of despair
I have cried out in the night for relief
I have suffered like you

I know it seems utterly impossible that it will pass
I know it seems like your life is over
I know it feels so unfair to carry this woe
I know it feels like the bleeding will never cease

Then by the grace of G-d a hand appears
The prayers that you chanted in the darkness were received
The hours of unrelenting anguish are reduced to mere minutes
The weight of grief lifts

You begin to feel a state of calm
The soul radiates healing
The heart is soothed with rest
The brow is lighter

That is when the pain goes away
That is when you reclaim hope
That is when the heart heals

Pain is temporary
What you resist persists

The Unwilling Puppet

He was the new kid in town
He had a swagger in his step not of conceit but of confidence
He was chosen for what he had done in numerous locations

He spent his early days learning the ropes, shaking hands
He was always gracious
His word was his bond
His got things done

Then in time he got it built
He created a place in the community where people would gather
It was center for health and well being
Both the young and old would embrace it

They were still those who were not satisfied with his work
Despite his fearless commitment
They started to conjure a plot
To diminish this fine man

So they assaulted him with gossip
The attempted to discredit his character
They were in fact jealous

He took the high rode
He had every reason to retaliate
But that was not his style
Always by his side she stood

So he devised a plan to exit with grace and class
He headed for the door
Placed the keys on the counter
He cut the strings

Pyramid Lake, NY

A Man in a Cabin

I sequestered myself from the world
If for only a few days to gather my wits
The location was simple
It is a place of special meaning
For over two decades a favorite haunt

Of all the places to bunk
I chose the house on the hill
A small square box with the basic necessities
Four walls with a sturdy roof
A comfortable bed and a round table to write

A red candle flickered in the corner
Its radiance reinforces my being
It helps me understand where I have been
As distant fear scatters across the floor
I feel safe

I no longer fear the darkness
I cry at times as I touch the depth of my soul
I pay attention to all that I feel
So much pain
So much heart ache
So much intrusion of my personnel space

Things happened to this man in the cabin
Things happen to all of us
The joyous along with the devastation

All that matters is how we endure
All that matters is how we feel
We all matter

To Love

Just let me love one last time
Not like the first time

To love not with blind innocence
But with a heart which knows wisdom

Just let me love one last morning
With a rebirth of dedication to commitment

Just let me love one last evening
With a sense of mystery and passion

Just let me love one last time before
While I can experience unconditional love

Just one more time

Death

It is those five letters that unnerve us
They cause us great fear based upon uncertainty

Death with find us all sooner or later
There is little we can do to escape it
It will track us down
It will out run us
It will find our hiding places

So embracing our fate
Gives us a great freedom
A choice to live

To celebrate every day
No matter the weather
No matter the season
No matter the brightest sunshine
No matter the darkest night

To accept the inevitable
Is to celebrate the unlimited possibilities
What is your choice?
The clock is ticking
Time waits for no one
Not even you

Aphasia

I am afraid that I will never find the words
The words that came so spontaneously

I am afraid that I won't be able to express myself
That the thoughts that live deep inside have faded away

I am afraid that the experiences I had disappeared
That the pain, sorrow and recovery has vanished

As much as I try, I cannot find the key
The key to unlock those moments of change

Maybe the time spent alone from the world
In the darkness and quiet will allow for renewed meaning

Maybe the winter's cold will help my heart warm
The heat will stoke the fires of expression

Maybe I am in a place on hold
A temporary place of recovery

I will stand still
The moments will guide me

Words

I am afraid that I will never find the words
The words that came so spontaneously

I am afraid that I won't be able to express myself
That the thoughts that live deep inside have faded away

I am afraid that the experiences I had disappeared
That the pain, sorrow and recovery has vanished

As much as I try, I cannot find the key
The key to unlock those moments of change

Maybe the time spent alone from the world
In the darkness and quiet will allow for renewed meaning

Maybe the winter's cold will help my heart warm
The heat will stoke the fires of expression

Maybe I am in a place on hold
A temporary place of recovery

I will stand still
The moments will guide me

Blind

How can one have perfection vision
Yet be so blind

How can one point out the smallest of imperfections
Yet be unaware of the elephant in the room

How can one stand in front of the mirror
Yet be oblivious that one's hair is on fire

It is so effortless to point the finger at another
At times more than ten is needed to offend

What's makes a society enjoy the art of judgment?

They seem to be incapable of self-awareness
To be unable to go inside and reflect
To admit to short comings
To own one's behavior
To resist the temptation to attack others

It is possible to journey within
It is possible to look in the mirror
It is possible to change one's ways

To own what is yours
Is to embrace the winds of change

Hannah Ruth Foster
(Stanley's Granddaughter) c 1996

It's Free

On a beautiful afternoon I give you a flower
It grows tall in the radiant sunlight
The pedals bob and sway in the ocean breeze

You clutch it tightly in your tiny hand
You draw it near to inhale its beauty
Your eyes sparkle making you giggle

I want you to have it, as it reminds me of you
Full of goodness, an abundance of joy
To treasure it with everlasting memories
Find every simple gift
A glistening star
A radiant rainbow
A hand to hold

You are free to receive

Love at 3:00 am

So what is love?
Besides four letters connected

Many prophets, poets and sages have attempted to explain
There appears to be no definitive answer
Maybe love has many dimensions
So allow me my two cents

Love is the basis for human existence
Love comes with no guarantees
Love consoles the wounded heart
Love stokes the fire of passion
Love is a harbor during rough seas
Love is a warm blanket
Love is a contoured mug filled with warm coffee
Love is ability to forgive AND forget
Love is free, no funds to exchange
Love is an umbrella on a rainy day
Love is a hand to hold
Love moves the hair off the brow
Love is without judgement
Love is answering the call anytime
Love has many colors
Love is a home cooked meal
Love is anything made by hand
Love is a calm voice in the night
Love is home to where you are
Love is the look of adoration and desire
Love can be unspoken
Love shouldn't cost you a thing

Without love the heart will cease to beat
Without love, death is more certain sooner than later

The Victim

To be a victim is to sign up and volunteer
To be a victim is to self-injure
A victim holds yourself hostage

Feeling the pain of
Disappointment.....betrayal.....loss.....deception.....abandonment
Is perfectly relevant to the human condition
But one must set the timer to be free to:
Rage.....stomp.....emote.....spew.....howl.....weep.....

To construct a documentary or mini-series of suffering
Serves little purpose in the process of healing

So set a timer
Create a concrete end
The continuous victim is a bore
Failing to quiet their ego

In Time

I can only write what I know
I can only express what I feel
I can only dream of what I desire

I have lost her again
It all came so quickly
Barely able to hear the door close before I fell to ground
I couldn't catch my breath as all substances drained from me

How could this happen again?
Did I lose focus? Was I not paying attention?
I quickly blamed myself as to have not doing enough
I questioned all my motives

And then others voices found me
They stated the quality of my character
The commitment in my words
The ability to give with my heart fully exposed

So now I have the time to heal
I make the time to reflect without self-injury
I take pause in all those lovely moments
Which have now all gone away
It is in fact a death, worthy of mourning

In time the days will be less long
In time the nights will calm
In time I will ache less
In time, not my time

Stanley (c. 1945)

Hand in Hand

She stayed long enough so I could care for myself
I watch her from the foot of the bed, she is on her way
Her bags are already packed, ticket in hand

As she moves towards the light he awaits her
In the distance she sees a silhouette
A lean figure with a radiate head of hair

As she moves closer that boyish smile sparkles
He reaches out his hand in assurance
He states that she is safe and all is well
All her worries have evaporated like the morning dew

She takes his hand, gazing with utter delight
Towards the light that move
To live in eternal peace

Grace Foster

State of Grace

They took their usual Sunday stroll hand in hand
The fallen leaves beneath their feet gave them a colorful carpet
The trail wrapped around the still lake the
chilled breeze reddened their cheeks

They stopped briefly to feel the moment
Close by they heard a quiet whimpering
They made their way to a mighty oak naked in appearance

At the foot of the tree they found a small bird relocated from the nest
This tiny creature was calling out for help with all its might
So the couple instinctually scooped up the tiny bird and brought it home

The couple had two other mouths feed at home
but one more wasn't a problem
The couple had plenty of love for another
This young bird was too weak to fly
She required warmth, support, encouragement and unconditional love

Over time this divine being became stronger
She was determined to keep up with here elders
They motivated her to chart her own course
Her "parents" were always there to pick her up
They were a constant in all types of weather

Today this tiny being had blossomed
She soars high in the sky
She stands proudly with confidence and wisdom

Very soon she will leave the nest take flight to the east
So much awaits her
So many opportunities

So fly high with Grace

An Unexpected Gift

It wasn't even my birthday nor a special holiday
She would be last person in the world I would expect anything from
She took so much from me
I was left barren......out of tears......feeling hopeless

The gift sat in my house for days
I didn't have the strength to untie the bow and open the paper
As each day passed I summoned the energy

I opened the box and was reminded of what I had given
Not to provide to get something in return
More so to give unconditionally
I simply could not help myself, it is who I am

To love another human being means to do whatever needs to be done
To display one's humanity is the core of a loving relationship
I was so busy doing
That I lost myself as her servant

So as days past since her unexpected "death"
I was given time to spend time with this gift
Each day became less of a struggle
The darkness of night was balanced with the sunshine of the day

I have spent my time with me
I started to come back to myself
I took the time to sit in silence
No matter how painful
To emote my tears and to purge the pain

So each day I cherish her gift
Amen !!

Stanley's Son

News Flash

I recently heard we are all going to die
Not sure when
Not sure how
Please do not inform me ahead of time

Well now that we have that out of the way
What shall we do with ourselves?
How should we make the very best of our days?

The answer lies with our choices
You want be unhappy?
You want spend each moment complaining?
You want to spend each day whining?
You want to spend each day in an envious stupor?

Or

You want to love with reckless abandon
You want to laugh till you pee your pants
You want to say "I have enough"
You want to leave the past behind you
You want to live in the present
You want to dispose of your anger

So

It is quite simple
It is up to you
And only you

Friday Prayer

Just today guide me through the darkness
Hold me up when I fall
Help me realize after the showers fade a rainbow appears

Keep me in the day
Help me enjoy all the gifts I have
Keep me in your heart
I pray that my hard work
Will allow me to weather the storm

May my tears be sign of my healing heart
May each day give me hope

Joe P

He was a man that love the wilderness
The great outdoors was his play ground
He took many a trek off the beaten path

Always carrying just what he needed
A heavy pack filled with essentials
A walking stick in hand
And a gleeful strut in his stride

His journeys took him to the west
To experience the high peaks and low valleys
He was in awe to where his feet would take him

Then without an invitation he was overcome
His health had faded
His feet were tired
His clock was winding down

One last visit he made to Pyramid Lake
A lush garden of wilderness
In the circle he gave his farewells

His only request was to spread his spirit in the still waters
In the following spring, his wish was granted
I was blessed to able to set him free

His spirit forever flows

Bella Foster (c. 2014)

Mom's Day

For three trimesters they kept us safe
Providing comfort, nourishment and a haven
They carried us and took us everywhere

When we entered the world we saw them first
We were instantly showered with love
It flowed so naturally like the great falls after the winter thaw

As we grew, they were always there to tend to our needs
When we fell they scooped us up with comfort and reassurance
When we were unsure of ourselves they were our cheerleader

Their experiences was born out of their own childhood
We benefitted from their hopes, fears and challenges
Sometimes through osmosis they felt what we felt

We will only have one MOM
We may have not chosen them
But they do the best they can with what they have

Not just on the designated day
Let us always honor this eternal bond
Their unconditional love
Our relationship with mom
Is the fiber of our lives

Outing Myself

The truth is I can really sing
The other truth I can really dance

If you ask me to I will tell you no
If you ask me twice my answer is still no

There are things best left to be imagined
There some moments just to be cherished alone

It is not about being selfish
It more about honoring one self
It is about letting it all go

The voice
The movement
The joy
It is a personnel celebration

Hate

It is the most powerful word in the English language
How four adjoining letters can impact civilizations?

The is no calculator that can hold all the numbers
For all that have perished from hate

The intensity of the feeling causes men to foam
The physiological changes are many

Seething
Gritting teeth
Hair on end
Tightness
Glazed eyes
Yelling
Raging
Black out
Violence

Some are so overcome their voices spew fire
Their words reflect deep rage
Their emotions are like a runaway train
They seek punishment, retribution, blame and even death

When intoxicated under the influence of hate
There exists a complete absence of awareness
The virtual cluelessness that the owner of hate possesses
As he drives down the road of perdition
Or choses to drink from the river of Styx
What you hate and who you hate always goes unscathed
It is the most deadly self-inflicted wound

A hater cannot find their way out of the abyss

The best antidote for hate is love
To love one-self is to be worthy of disappointment and betrayal
Say "hi" to poor me for a second then send it on its way

When you send hate from your house
Open the door and invite love into your heart

Wickford, RI

Enough

A warm blanket
A roof over your head
A hand to hold
Food to satisfy your hunger
A drink to quench your thirst
A warm embrace
A shoulder to cry on
Laughter that hurts your belly
A dependable car
Your good health
Unconditional love from your partner
Infinite kisses
A friend that always takes your call

Isn't that all u need?
Isn't that enough?

If you find yourself continually seeking more
If you have a habit of comparing to others
Maybe you are not enough
For you will never fill the need with tangible things
No amount of cash can buy you fulfillment

It is strictly and inside job

Lake Provence, NH

Recover

By the still waters begins the healing
The constant ebb and flow is a cadence for my soul
I have been challenged by unexpected events
My body has been battered and beaten
A series of unrelenting experiences

My will keeps telling me to move forward
My body has its own agenda
It is time for me to take time
To withdraw from the daily routine

So I step away with uncertainty
I am unaccustomed to sitting idle
I find a nap to be a luxury

I ease into this new life a day at a time
I seek the calm from within
I allow the brow to fall
I permit my jaw to relax

I seek a place of calm and serenity
I am akin to the water
The constant force of time
The methodic beat of my spirit

Where this course takes me is uncertain
I choose to surrender
To let it go under the universe's plan

May I find my direction by the water's edge
Gaining confidence from the powerful falls
To feel the cleansing spray
Anointing my weary body

Drunkard

I was never one to take for drink
Maybe now and then
But then I found something more intoxicating
A strong connection to another being

It was not just about desire and passion
It was a feeling of joy and comfort
The location nor space we shared did not matter

It was a state of bliss
What fool wouldn't want to experience that?
Maybe I became addicted
Maybe I found what had been missing for so long

And then she went away
My withdrawals left me with the shakes
My gait was impaired
A tsunami of tears
I sought counsel to make sense of it all

As the days pass I am unsure if I miss her
Rather that I miss the elation in my heart

Printed in the United States
By Bookmasters